COO 121 274X

D0708451

Reptiles

Anita Ganeri

Watts Books
London • New York • Sydney

Watts Books
96 Leonard Street
London EC2A 4RH

Franklin Watts Australia
14 Mars Road
Lane Cove
NSW 2066

UK ISBN: 0 7496 1573 7

10 9 8 7 6 5 4 3 2 1

Dewey Decimal Classification 597.9

Series editor: Pippa Pollard
Editor: Jane Walker
Design: Visual Image
Artwork: Mainline Design
Cover artwork: Mainline Design
Photo research: Alison Renwick
Fact checking: Simone K. Lefolii

A CIP catalogue record for this book is available from the British Library

Printed in Italy by
G. Canale & C. SpA

Contents

What are reptiles?

When you think of a **reptile**, you probably think of a snake or a lizard. Crocodiles and tortoises are reptiles, too. No matter how different reptiles look, they all share some special features. They have a bony **skeleton** inside their body and scaly skin. They all breathe air through lungs. Most reptiles lay eggs on land.

▽ All reptiles have scaly skin. A gecko's skin is brightly coloured.

All kinds of reptiles

There are reptiles of all shapes and sizes, from huge, dragon-like lizards to snakes that are thinner than pencils. Reptiles can be split up into different groups. The five main groups are snakes, lizards, turtles and tortoises, crocodiles and alligators, and tuataras. All together, there are more than 6,000 different types of reptile in the world.

▽ The Komodo dragon is a gigantic lizard. It is 3 metres long and can swallow a pig whole.

▷ Tortoises are easy to recognise by their hard shells.

△ The least gecko is one of the smallest reptiles. It grows to about 5 centimetres long.

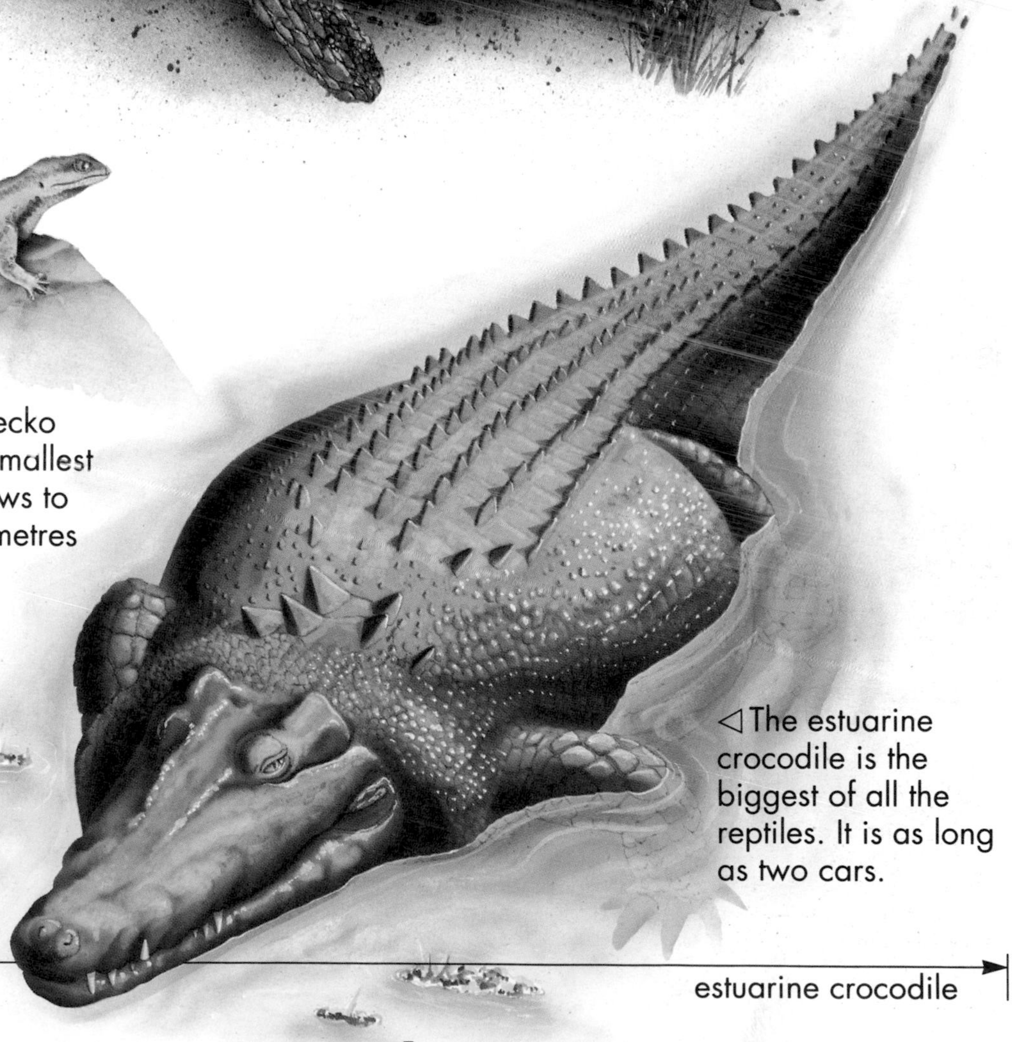

◁ The estuarine crocodile is the biggest of all the reptiles. It is as long as two cars.

gecko

estuarine crocodile

Where do reptiles live?

Most reptiles live on land – in forests, in deserts and even in people's homes. Some, such as turtles and sea snakes, spend most of their life in the sea or in rivers. Reptiles like living in warm places. This is because they are **cold-blooded** animals. Their bodies do not work well in cold weather. They need to warm up in the sun first.

▷The emerald tree boa climbs trees to look for food. It wraps itself around the branches.

▽ Sea turtles spend most of their life in the sea. They only come ashore to lay their eggs.

◁ Fringe-toed lizards look as if they are dancing on the hot desert sand. In fact, they lift up their feet to let the air cool them.

▷ Most crocodiles live in and around rivers and muddy swamps.

Food for reptiles

Most reptiles eat meat. They eat all sorts of other animals and other reptiles. Crocodiles and alligators have sharp teeth for catching and eating their food. Komodo dragons have teeth with **serrated** edges, like knives. Tortoises and some large lizards mainly eat plants. Sea snakes eat fish, but some sea turtles eat fish and sea plants.

▷ A chameleon catches insects by shooting out its long sticky tongue at them.

▽ Tortoises are too slow to chase other animals to eat. They mainly munch on plants.

▽ When a crocodile's old teeth wear out, a new set is ready to take their place.

Snake snacks

Snakes eat birds, lizards, mice and bigger animals, such as deer and pigs. Smaller snakes eat birds' eggs, snails and slugs. Some snakes kill their **prey** with poison (see page 12). Others squeeze their prey to death. Snakes cannot bite or chew so they swallow their food whole. One large meal can last a snake for weeks or even months on end.

▽ Egg-eating snakes swallow eggs whole, eat the insides and spit out the shells.

▽ A python can kill an animal as big as a gazelle. It may take the snake a week to digest the gazelle.

△ A snake can swallow its prey whole because it has very stretchy jaws.

Fangs and poisons

Many snakes use poison to kill their prey and to protect themselves from their enemies. The most poisonous snakes are cobras, sea snakes and vipers. They inject their poison through special teeth, called **fangs**. There are also two types of poisonous lizard – the gila monster and the Mexican beaded lizard.

▷The king cobra rears up and spreads out its hood, ready to strike its prey.

▽ The spitting cobra spits poison into its enemy's eyes.

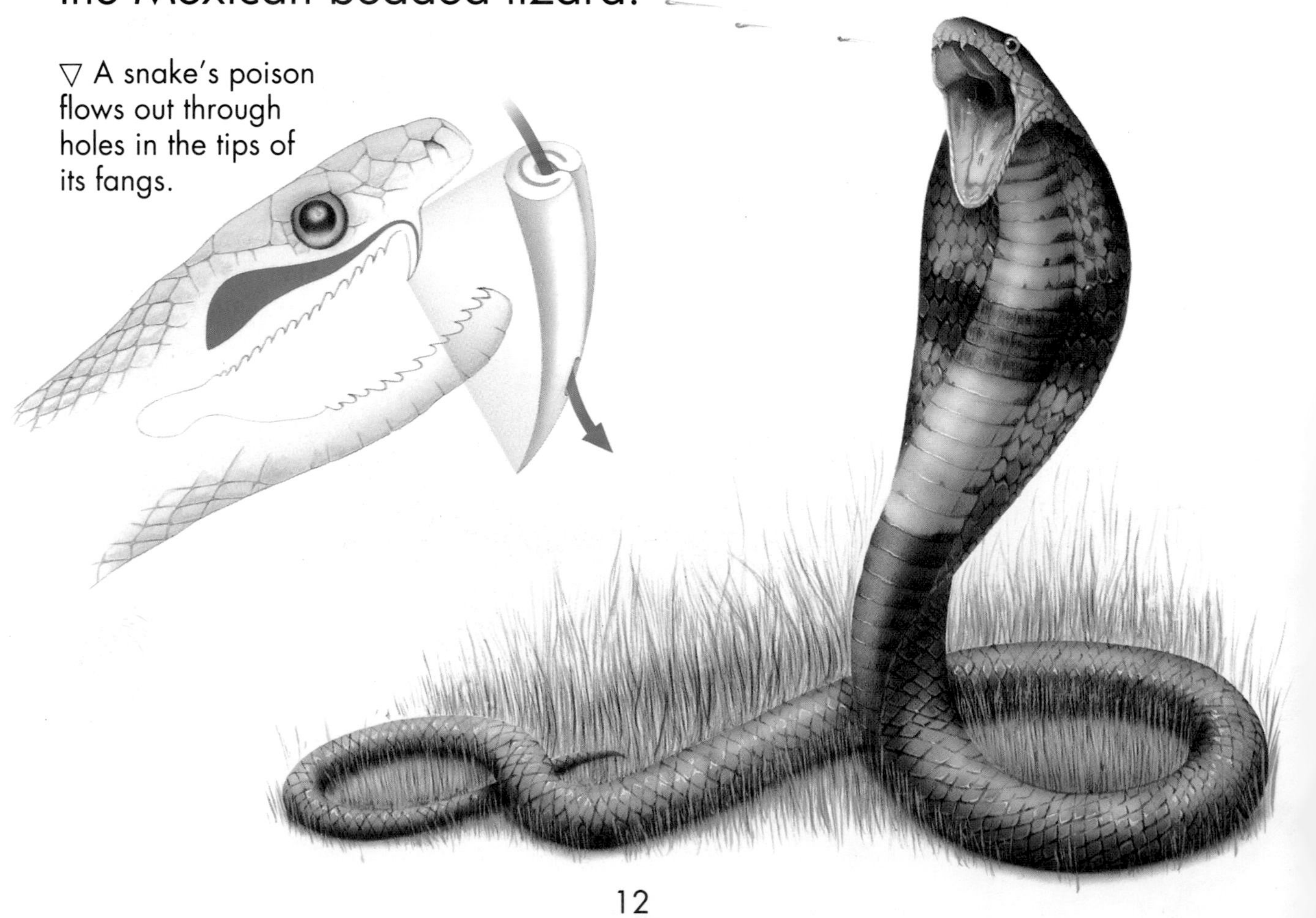

▽ A snake's poison flows out through holes in the tips of its fangs.

▽ The gila monster does not have fangs. Poison trickles down grooves on its teeth.

Skins and scales

All reptiles have dry, scaly skin. The **scales** are made from thick patches of skin. They stop the reptiles drying out in the heat. They also protect the reptiles from attack and wear and tear. From time to time, reptiles shed their old, worn-out skins and grow new ones. This gives them room to grow bigger.

▽ The thorny moloch lizard has sharp spikes on its skin. These help to scare off attackers.

▷ Snakes crawl out of their old skins, leaving them behind in one piece.

◁Caimans, crocodiles and alligators have strong armour plates on their backs. These are made from scales and bone.

Staying alive

Reptiles have many enemies, including bigger animals, other reptiles and people. They also have many ways of defending themselves. Some try running away at first, as fast as they can. If this does not work, some reptiles use special weapons or ways of behaving. Others use colours and patterns to hide from attackers.

▷The tail of the stump-tailed lizard is the same shape as its head. The lizard's enemies do not know which end of the lizard to attack.

▷Some snakes, like grass snakes, hiss and puff if attacked. This hog-nosed snake is pretending to be dead.

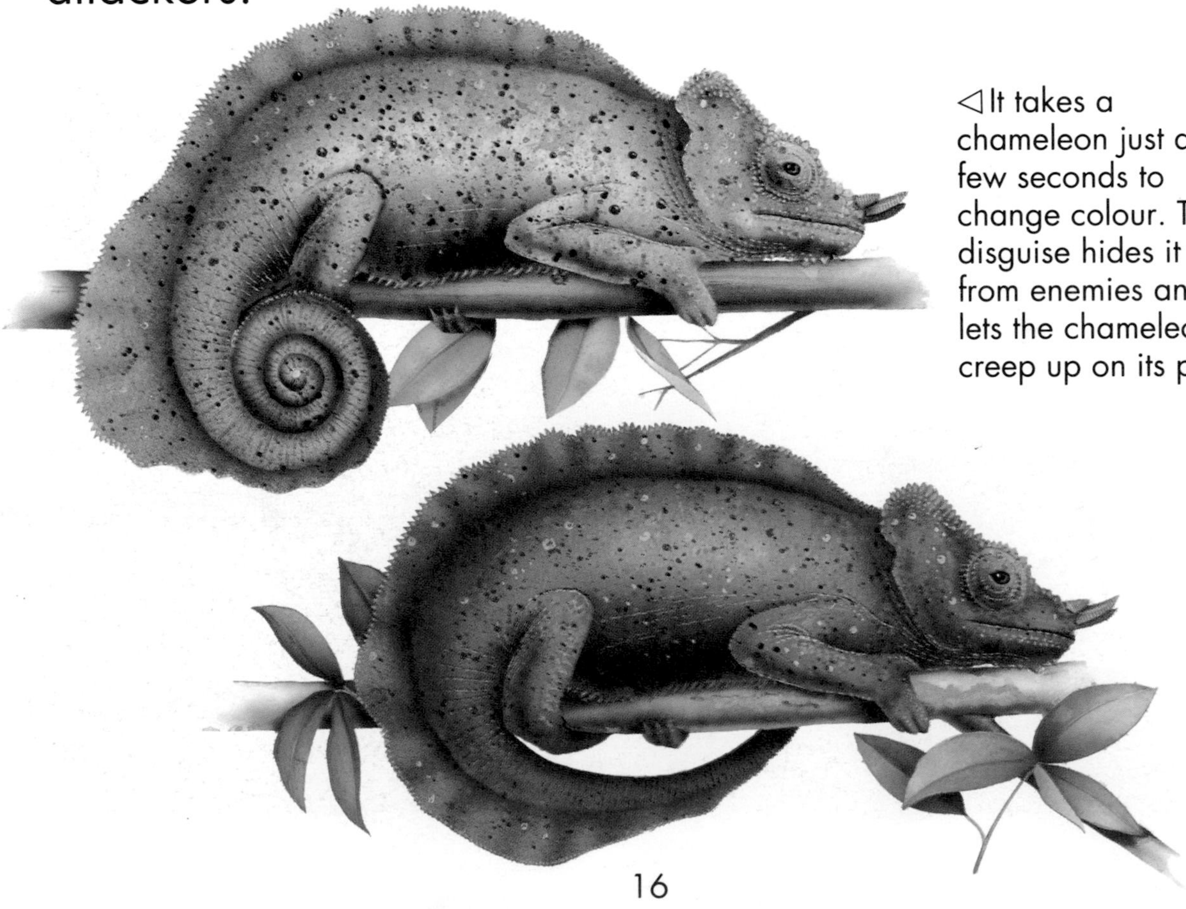

◁It takes a chameleon just a few seconds to change colour. This disguise hides it from enemies and lets the chameleon creep up on its prey.

▽ The Australian frilled lizard spreads out the frill of skin around its neck to scare away its enemies.

Eggs and babies

Most baby reptiles hatch out of eggs. The eggs are usually laid on land, in nests made of plants or mud, or in holes in the ground. Most reptile eggs have soft, bendy shells. But crocodiles, tortoises and many geckos lay eggs with hard shells, like birds' eggs. Some parents guard their nests until the eggs hatch. Then the young reptiles have to look after themselves.

▷ These newly hatched baby turtles are making their way to the sea on their own.

▽ Baby tortoises have a special spike on their nose, called an egg tooth. They use this to break through their egg shells.

▽ Sea turtles lay their eggs in holes on a sandy beach.

▽ An Indian python coils her body around her eggs to keep them warm until they hatch.

Roaming reptiles

The way a reptile moves depends on where it lives. Reptiles which live in the sea or near rivers are good swimmers. Turtles use their strong front legs as paddles to push their bodies through the water. Reptiles which live in forests are good climbers. Their feet have sharp claws for gripping the trees. On the ground, tortoises are well known for being very slow movers.

▷Geckos can climb up walls and walk upside down on the ceiling. Their feet have pads of tiny hairs to grip.

▽ The basilisk lizard races across the surface of the water on its wide feet. If it slows down, it will fall in.

◁ Marine iguanas swim in the sea to find seaweed to eat.

▷ The six-lined racerunner is the fastest reptile on land. Its top speed is 29 kilometres per hour, which is about four times faster than your normal walking pace.

Slithering snakes

Snakes do not have legs so they cannot run or walk about like other reptiles. Instead, they **slither** across the ground using their strong muscles to push and pull them along. Some snakes are also good at climbing and swimming. When they slither or climb, they use their scales for extra grip.

▷The black mamba is the fastest-moving snake.

▽ Some snakes move by bunching their bodies up, then stretching out again.

▽ Sidewinder snakes move in loops across the sand.

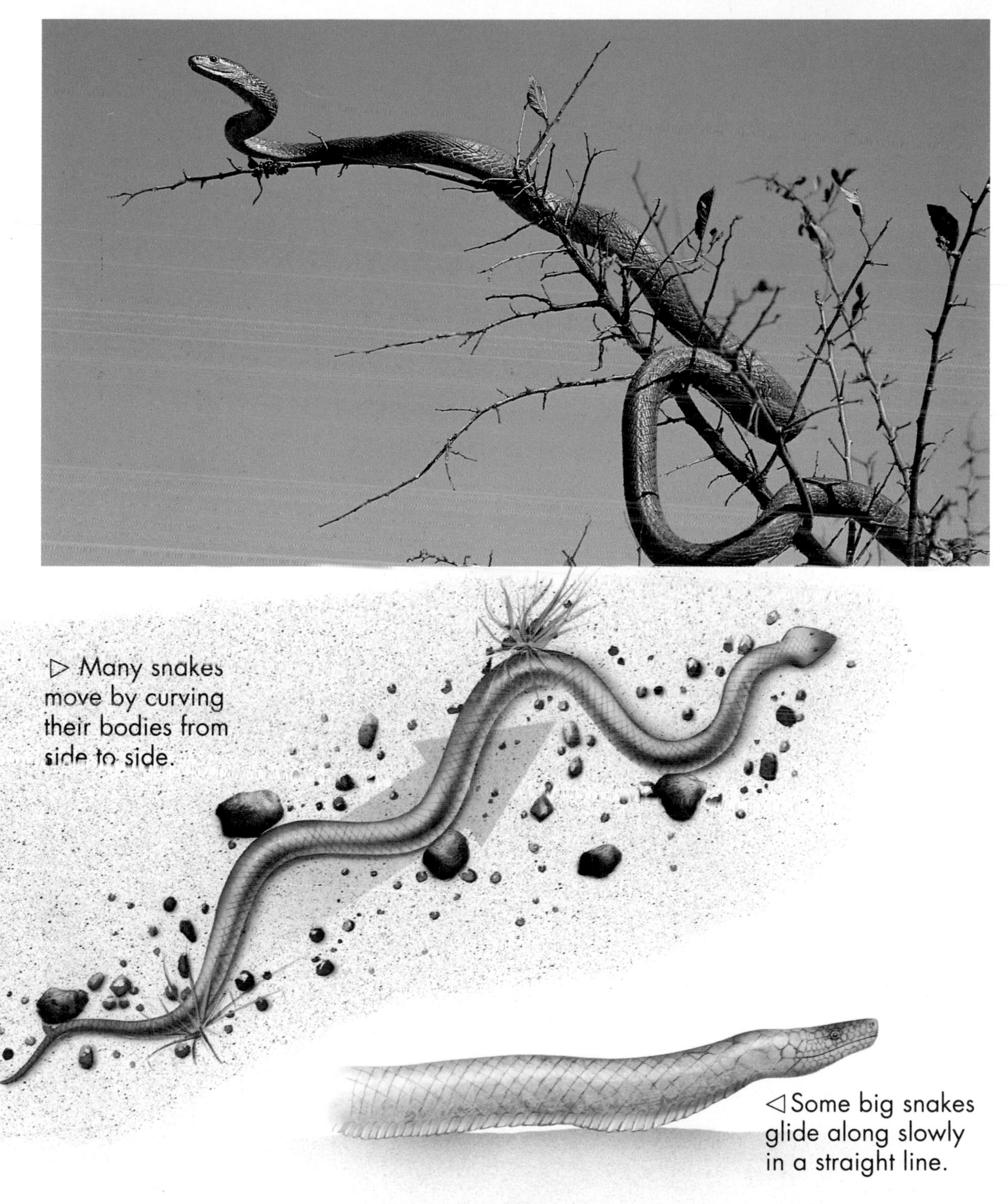

▷ Many snakes move by curving their bodies from side to side.

◁ Some big snakes glide along slowly in a straight line.

Reptile senses

Reptiles have some special **senses** which help them to find out what is happening in the world around them. Snakes do not have ears and cannot hear very well. But they pick up sounds from the ground through their skull bones. Lizards and snakes 'smell' things with their **forked** tongues. They flick them in and out to pick up smells from the air.

▷A chameleon can move each eye on its own. It can look in two different directions at the same time.

▽ This monitor lizard is 'smelling' the air with its tongue.

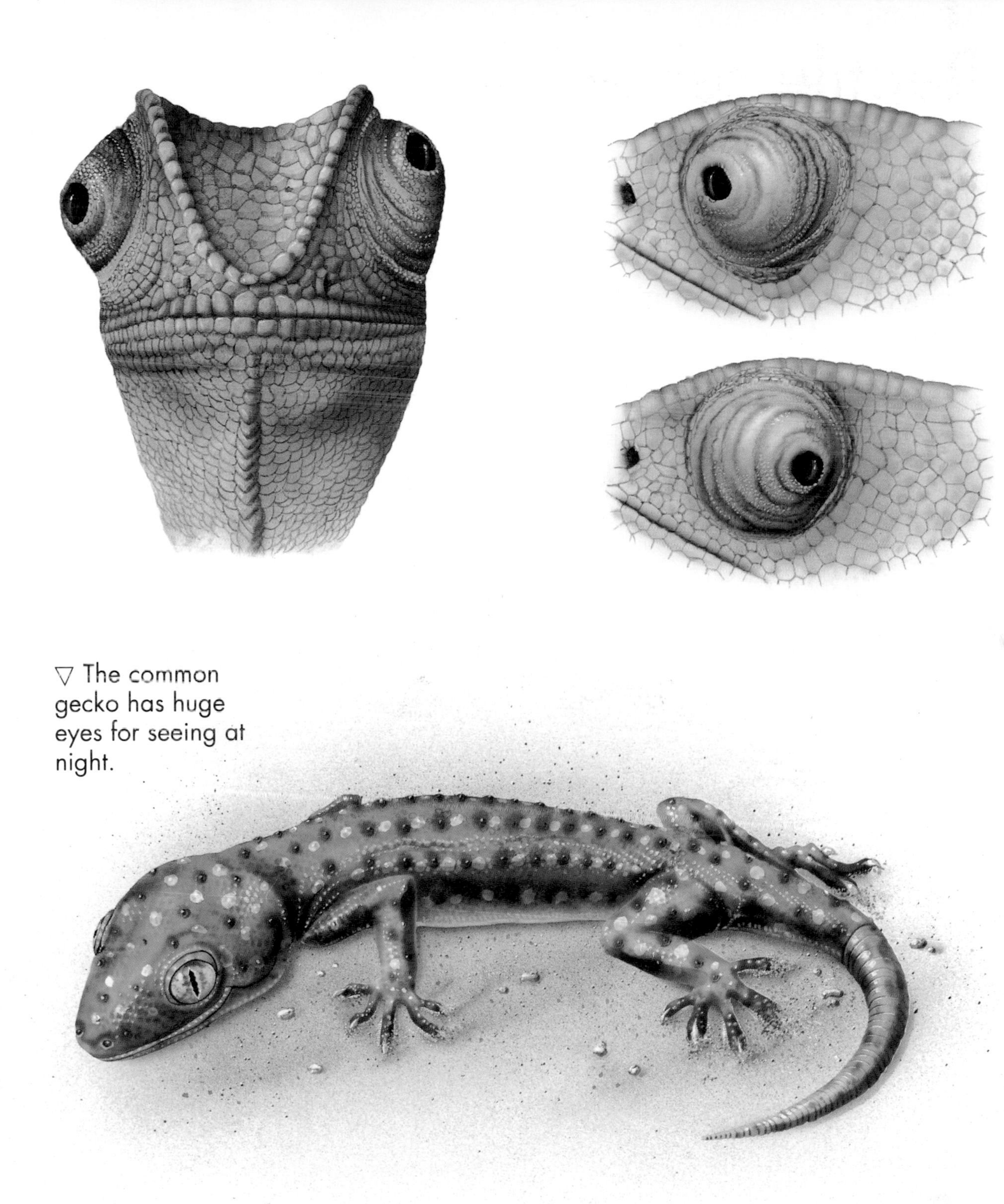

▽ The common gecko has huge eyes for seeing at night.

Related to reptiles

The most famous reptiles of all are the mighty dinosaurs. They appeared on Earth about 220 million years ago and died out about 65 million years ago. Other **prehistoric** reptiles included the **pterosaurs**, which lived in the sea and the sky. There were also reptiles which looked like the ones we know today. The first snakes lived on Earth over 100 million years ago.

▷ Pteranodons flapped through the prehistoric skies on leathery wings.

▽ The ichthyosaurus was a prehistoric sea reptile which looked like a dolphin.

▷ The strange tuatara lives in New Zealand. It is the only survivor of a group of reptiles which lived millions of years ago.

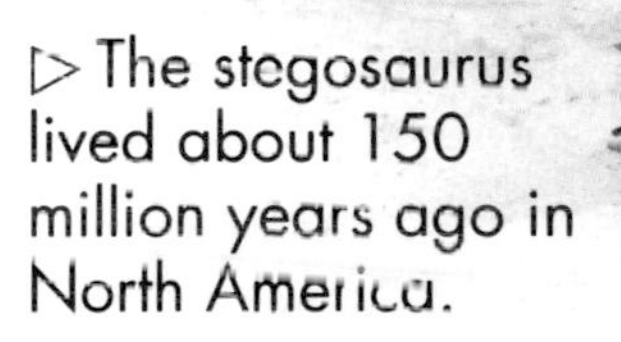

▷ The stegosaurus lived about 150 million years ago in North America.

Reptiles at risk

Many of today's reptiles are in danger of becoming **extinct**, like the dinosaurs. Their worst enemies are human beings. People kill snakes, lizards and alligators for their skins. Turtles are killed for their meat and eggs. People are also destroying the reptiles' homes in the wild. Many of the rarest reptiles are now protected by special laws.

▷ These caimans have been killed and stuffed. They are then sold as souvenirs.

▽ Giant tortoises live on the Galapagos Islands. Some types of giant tortoise are already extinct.

◁ Reptiles have natural enemies, too. Among a cobra's worst enemies is the fierce little mongoose.

Things to do

If you are interested in reptiles and would like to know more about them, there are lots of places you can write to for information. Here are a few useful addresses:

British Herpetological Society
c/o The Zoological Society of London
Regents Park
LONDON
NW1 4RY

This society studies European reptiles and amphibians (e.g. frogs and toads).

World Wide Fund for Nature (WWF)
Panda House
Weyside Park
GODALMING
Surrey
GU7 1XR

The WWF is trying to save endangered animals, including reptiles, all over the world.

Watch
c/o The Royal Society for Nature Conservation (RSNC)
22 The Green
Nettleham
LINCOLN
LN2 2NR

A conservation group especially for young people.

Friends of the Earth
26–28 Underwood Street
LONDON
N1 7JQ

This organisation is trying to protect the environment and the animals living in it.

Glossary

cold-blooded Depends on the sun to get warm. When cold-blooded animals warm up their bodies in the sun, they become more active. In cold weather they are slow and sluggish.

extinct No longer exists on the Earth. Animals which are extinct have all died out, like the dinosaurs.

fangs Special teeth through which snakes squirt poison into their enemies or into their prey.

forked Split into two prongs at one end.

prehistoric Prehistoric animals are those that lived before history began.

prey Animals which are hunted as food by other animals.

pterosaur A prehistoric flying reptile which lived about 200 million years ago.

reptile An animal with a skeleton and a scaly skin. It breathes air, and most lay eggs on land. Snakes, lizards, tortoises and crocodiles are reptiles.

scales Thick, extra-tough patches of skin which cover a reptile's body. They protect its body and stop it drying out in the heat.

senses The ways in which animals find out about the world around them. The five senses are smell, sight, taste, touch and hearing.

serrated Jagged, like the blade of a saw.

shed To lose or get rid of. Many reptiles shed their old, worn-out skins.

skeleton The framework of bones inside a reptile's body.

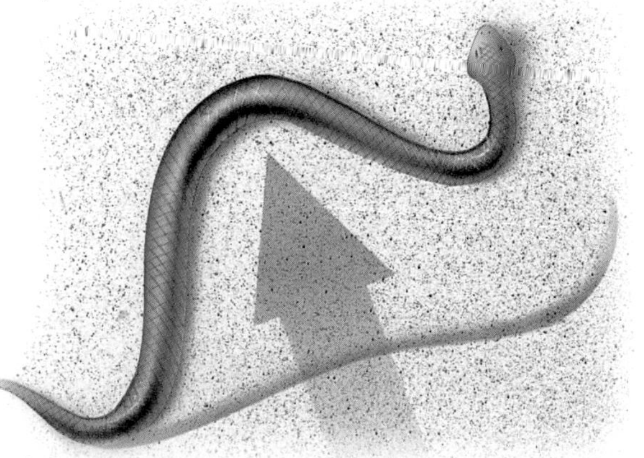

slither To move along the ground by slipping and sliding.

Index

Photographic credits:
Bruce Coleman Ltd 4, (K Taylor) 9;
NHPA (ANT) 17, 24, 27,
(A Bannister) 15, 19, 23,
(J Carmichael Jr) 7,
(S Dalton) 9, 20,
(G Gainsburgh) 3,
(E Hanumantha Rao) 13,
(D Heuclin) 10,
(M Wendler) 29.